Come Out of Hiding

Activating Deliverance

Christina Chislom

Acknowledgements

To my Creator, God, who sent his Son to die just for me. To Yeshua, who is alive with all power. To Holy Spirit, who guides me.

To my loving and supportive parents, William and Charlene Chislom, I share respect, gratitude, and love. And also to my brothers, William and Nick Chislom, my favorite guys!

To Apostle Wayman Thomas (Evelyn Thomas), thank you for Apostolic impartation, birthing, and fanning the apostolic and prophetic flames of fire inside of me.

A special Thank you to my Overseer, Apostle Darren Thomas (Pastor Sonya Thomas). Without your guidance, help, and dedication in pushing me to Build It In Public, this book would have remained locked up on the inside of me. Your spirit of creativity and excellence challenges me to thrive and not merely survive. *Todah Rabah Sir!*

To all my friends who have and are yet coming out of hiding; You are already loved!!!

And to all those who will read this book as you strive to be delivered and set free, you shall come forth!

COME OUT OF HIDING:
Activating Deliverance

TABLE OF CONTENTS

To Book Prophetess Christina in your city for book readings, prayer gatherings, conferences, women's events and more, or, to order additional copies of this book, please visit www.prophetesschristina.org.

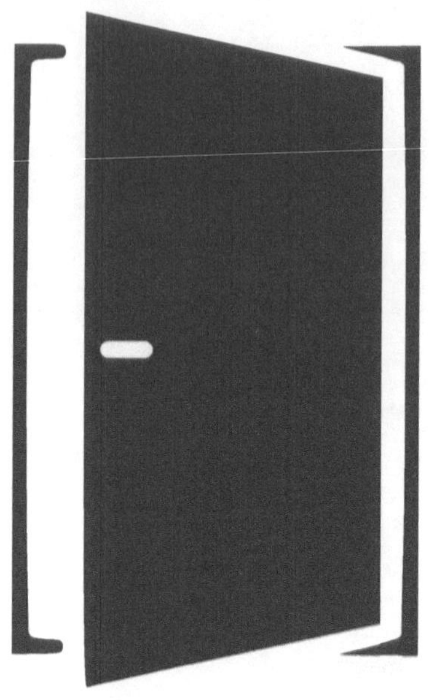

CHAPTER ONE

Come Out of Hiding

"Can anyone hide from me in a secret place?
Am I not everywhere in all the heavens and earth?"
says the LORD.

Jeremiah 23:24

Are you tired of living in bondage? Living with secrets,? Dealing with the feelings of shame, hurt, rejection, and fear? Are you tired of feeling like a failure? Or, tired of trying to come up with new lies to cover old lies? Are you tired of dealing with anxiety and intimidation? Is your struggle one of pride, or forgiveness? Perhaps your struggle is a sexual sin? Or masturbation? Or pornography? It may be one of bitterness, lust, or gluttony? Are you exhausted from these and other setbacks, personal issues, and bad habits? These behaviors will keep you operating under the system of bondage to sin and its master!

John 8:44 (NIV) states, "You belong to your father, the devil, and you want to carry out your father's desires. He was a murderer from the beginning, not holding to the truth, for there is no truth in him. When he lies, he speaks his native language, for he is a liar and the father of lies."

THIS IS YOUR DAY OF FREEDOM!

Even as you are reading this book right now, I declare to you, "This is your day of freedom!" Hallelujah! This is the perfect time to come out of hiding, expose what's been distracting you, and be free! Yeshua died that we all might be free. This includes you too!

Your adversary's strategy and plan is exposed in The Gospel of John 10:10. It reads, "The thief comes only to steal and kill and destroy; I have come that they may have life and have it to the full."

Today is your day. Now is your moment to become aware of the spirits hiding inside keeping you bound. It's time to make a demand for these strongholds to come out of hiding. YOU must make the demand and command these strongholds to let you go (mind, body, and spirit), so that you may be free.

A story that comes to mind where an encounter with Yeshua caused a nameless woman with many secrets to come out of Hiding. It's the story of the Woman at the Well. Her name was not given, but from the time her story was recorded in The Scriptures until now, a dynamic account of God's grace, compassion, boldness, and power to deliver us is displayed. There is no reason to hide from God. Freedom is engaged by coming out of hiding.

This story of the Woman at the Well is one studied by scholars for years. And while there is much revelation within this text, for the purpose of this book, I wish to deal with how her story relates to the need for deliverance.

The Gospel of John 4:4-26 (NOG) reads as thus,

4 Yeshua had to go through Samaria.

5 He arrived at a city in Samaria called Sychar. Sychar was near the piece of land that Jacob had given to his son Joseph.

6 Jacob's Well was there. Yeshua sat down by the well because he was tired from traveling. The time was about six o'clock in the evening.

7 A Samaritan woman went to get some water. Yeshua said to her, "Give me a drink of water." 8 (His disciples had gone into the city to buy some food.)

9 The Samaritan woman asked him, "How can a Jewish man like you ask a Samaritan woman like me for a drink of water?" (Jews, of course, don't associate with Samaritans.)

10 Yeshua replied to her, "If you only knew what God's gift is and who is asking you for a drink, you would have asked him for a drink. He would have given you living water."

11 The woman said to him, "Sir, you don't have anything to use to get water, and the well is deep. So where are you going to get this living water?

12 You're not more important than our ancestor Jacob, are you? He gave us this well. He and his sons and his animals drank water from it."

13 Yeshua answered her, "Everyone who drinks this water will become thirsty again.

14 But those who drink the water that I will give them will never become thirsty again. In fact, the water I will give them will become in them a spring that gushes up to eternal life."

15 The woman told Yeshua, "Sir, give me this water! Then I won't get thirsty or have to come here to get water."

16 Yeshua told her, "Go to your husband, and bring him here."

17 The woman replied, "I don't have a husband." Yeshua told her, "You're right when you say that you don't have a husband.

18 You've had five husbands, and the man you have now isn't your husband. You've told the truth."

19 The woman said to Yeshua, "I see that you're a prophet!

20 Our ancestors worshiped on this mountain. But you Jews say that people must worship in Jerusalem."

21 Yeshua told her, "Believe me. A time is coming when you Samaritans won't be worshiping the Father on this mountain or in Jerusalem.

22 You don't know what you're worshiping. We Jews know what we're worshiping, because salvation comes from the Jews.

23 Indeed, the time is coming, and it is now here, when the true worshipers will worship the Father in spirit and truth. The Father is looking for people like that to worship him.

24 God is a spirit. Those who worship him must worship in spirit and truth."

25 The woman said to him, "I know that the Messiah is coming. When he comes, he will tell us everything." (Messiah is the one called Christ.)

26 Yeshua told her, "I am he, and I am speaking to you now."

In verse nine we see the SPIRIT OF REJECTION in operation due to the fact that Yeshua being a Jew was not to associate with Samaritans. After all, they were thought of as outsiders and not to be brought close. In verse 12 we see the SPIRIT OF PRIDE and REJECTION working together as many spirits or strongholds often travel in pairs. Verses 16 through 18, Yeshua exposed her ADULTERY. Yeshua did not confront her to expose her. He confronted her to free her. It is the same with each of us. Yeshua knows what our struggle is and what we fight daily to overcome. He also knows what we hide. Thank God, He is full of compassion and ready to forgive and deliver us from what ever has us bound.

Next, in verse 28, the woman left her water jar. This represents her old profession. Her old lifestyle. Her old lovers. When she left her water jar, she fell out of or broke the agreement with her old nature. As a result, in verse 39,

LEARN TO BREAK THE AGREEMENT

many other Samaritans began to believe in Yeshua! This is what God desires to do with you! With each of us. Why are you waiting? You have family and friends who will be set free by your testimony!

This is a concise, yet powerful, deliverance handbook that will help you: 1) break free, 2) challenge all bad spirits to come out of hiding, and 3) discover the power that is alive and at work inside of you. This power will make you whole and set you free, indeed!

Come Out of Hiding is designed for mature believers who have found themselves bound in certain areas and in need of a tool to overcome some silent battles.

As you read this book, declare the prayers (listed later) as often as necessary. Engage daily steps towards your deliverance. As you do, you will begin to be set free!

A valuable part of being free is being able to share your testimony and no longer hide. The more you tell of your deliverance, the easier it is to remain free!

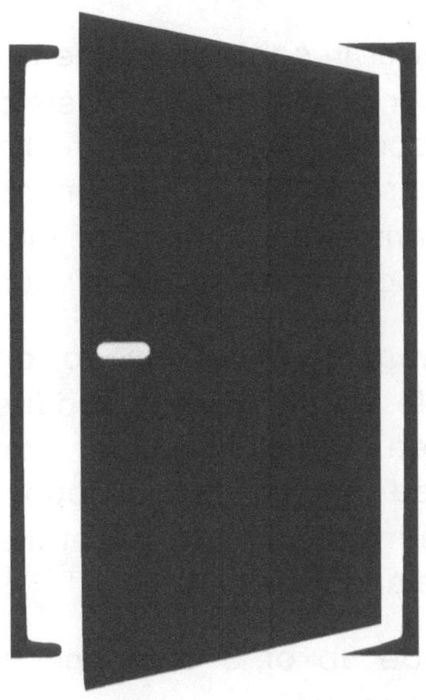

CHAPTER TWO

Fall Out Of Agreement With It

"Can two walk together unless
they have agreed to do so?"

Amos 3:3

There is power in confession, the bible says death and life are in the power of the tongue. Therefore, there is power in the words we speak. And, there are times when you are bound, that you must fall out of agreement with some habits, behaviors, addictions, sins, actions of the flesh, or anything that seems like its holding on strong in your life.

Demons want to hold on to anything they can concerning your life. As children of God it should be a strong desire to be set free from all bondage, strongholds, addictive behaviors and bad habits. In our body, soul and spirit. Deliverance is one major ways to target these areas and gain your freedom once and for all.

- Man is made up of 3 components: body, soul and spirit. (Hebrews 4:12)

- We are a spirit, that has a soul, that lives in a body. (Thessalonians 5:23; Obadiah 1:17)

- Deliverance – The action of being set free, body, mind, soul, and spirit.

When we talk about falling out of agreement, looking again at the woman at the well after her conversation with Yeshua, the scripture records around verse 28 that she left her water pot. This water pot could be her old profession, former lifestyle, that thing that brought her to a thirsty place, or even what connected her to sin. The thing that once mattered to her didn't really seem to matter anymore. When you make a decision to fall out of agreement with the past, your future and your freedom will mean more to you than anything that once had you bound. And once she encountered the One who walked on water she forgot she was thirsty!

Perhaps you are in agreement with some things simply because you don't know you are. Maybe you don't know how good it feels to be free? Think about some area in your life that has been hard to over come. Let's say, gossiping. Confess with your mouth to The Father today and declare, "I fall out of agreement with the spirit and actions of gossip. I no longer agree to give my time to something that is not feeding my life. In Yeshua's Name, Amen."

Make these kind of confessions and decide to fall out of agreement with the things, people, places, memories, and bad habits that are not producing positivity in your life. COMING out of Hiding exposes what lies beneath, and uncovers what lies within. You must become emotionally tired of being drained by hidden secrets, or, being bound. You must believe that YOU deserve to be free!

Let's look at Romans 7:15-25
> For I do not understand my own actions [I am baffled
> and bewildered by them]. I do not practice what I
> want to do, but I am doing the very thing I hate [and
> yielding to my human nature, my worldliness--my
> sinful capacity].
> Now if I habitually do what I do not want to do, [that
> means] I agree with the Law, confessing that it is
> good (morally excellent).
> So now [if that is the case, then] it is no longer I who
> do it [the disobedient thing which I despise], but the
> sin [nature] which lives in me.
> For the good that I want to do, I do not do, but I
> practice the very evil that I do not want.
> For I joyfully delight in the law of God in my inner self
> [with my new nature], but I see a different law and
> rule of action in the members of my body [in its
> appetites and desires], waging war against the law of
> my mind and subduing me and making me a prisoner
> of the law of sin which is within my members.

Wretched and miserable man that I am! Who will
[rescue me and] set me free from this body of death
[this corrupt, mortal existence]?
Thanks be to God [for my deliverance] through
YESHUA our Lord!
So then, on the one hand I myself with my mind
serve the law of God, but on the other, with my flesh
[my human nature, my worldliness, my sinful
capacity--I serve] the law of sin.

We must fall out of agreement with the laws of sin and death as believers. And agree with the law of God and come into the fullness of the freedom that comes by walking in the spirit, so we do not fulfill the lusts of the flesh.

In the previous text we see Paul writing a letter to the Romans. The Book of Romans is referred to by Chuck Swindoll, a prolific teacher of the word if God, as *'the corner stone of Christian truth."* He stated the Book of Romans helps us to understand our natural daily struggles, dealing with "the bottom line truth." Chuck said that many of the books in the new testament, including The Book of Romans are great books by which Christians should live. Especially the new believer.   I chose this text because Paul used the term agree.

To shed even more detailed light on falling out of agreement with something I will give a personal area I had to confront and overcome. This is one of many, but I want to provide an example. I too have to make declarations to stay free. And if I'm truly honest, when memories the enemy, or my emotions, began to [for whatever reason], come in like a flood, I verbally make a confession to come out of agreement with whatever it is trying to attach or 'reattach' itself to me, my emotions, or my actions and reactions.

FALL OUT OF AGREEMENT WITH IT

Love relationships is the example I will use. There were times I had to fall out of agreement with him, her, it, or them. I make that statement because I have had to fall out of agreement in many types of relationships: male love relationships, female love relationships, food relationships and others. Addiction is real, and has no gender preference. Addiction is a strong hold that will destroy you if you do not fight to break free. If I were to sift through every relationship I have been in, I would have to write an entirely different book. (Maybe I will get started on the next book entitled "fall out of agreement with the wrong one...")

I have been in some relationships that were not in God's plan for my life. And I say that because a relationship that is God-inspired will not hurt you, or damage your relationship with God. A God-inspired relationship will not involve fornication, perversion, lies, cheating, verbal, mental or emotional abuse. A God-inspired relationship will not produce a constant conviction that something is inappropriate. Whether the relationship lasts two months, six months, twelve months or 24 years, the longer you stay in a relationship that is unhealthy, the harder it will be to end it and heal from it.

One relationship I remember, in particular, was honestly both of our faults. Mental stress, other people on the side getting involved, lies, sex outside of marriage, and more. I was hurt, rejected, and did a lot of hiding. To face the fact that something needs to end is one thing. But to really end it and live life after a breakup is another ball game. And the break up process was hard, long, and at times, brutal. However, it is worth the peace of mind to completely heal and be free! In order to do that I had to learn to pray the prayer and make the confession to come out of Hiding and fall out of agreement with everything that was holding me hostage, especially In my mind, my will, and my emotions.

Honest confession to God goes a long way. He is fully aware of our mistakes, bad choices, short-comings, habits and relationships. When we invite Him in, and kick the devil out, healing will begin!

After a breakup you will feel sad, which can open you up for the spirit of depression which may have already been lurking, depending upon how bad the relationship was. Anxiety, fear, worry, stress, anger, hurt, the list can go on. You may have been previously rejected by someone and a breakup triggers feelings of hurt and rejection. The spirit of rejection likes to travel with friends. Low self esteem is one of them. (For more information on spirits and how they operate see Pigs in a Parlor. Frank and Ida Mae Hammond). My apostolic father had our church read that entire book. I guarantee it will shed light on some areas of bondage in your life.) You can also follow apostolic leaders such as Stephen Garner and John Eckhardt on YouTube and read their books to get more information on demonic spirits and how they function.

You may deal with loneliness, bitterness and unforgiveness. These are all spirits you must address by name and confess 'I fall out of Agreement with you'. Falling out of agreement with someone may even lead you to speak or declare a person by name. I had to do this in my own life. I had to say the person's name. Sometimes, you must be honest with yourself and accept the reality that you have not really let something or someone go. Being honest with yourself is key in breaking the tie.

Acceptance is the first step. This is not a one time occurrence. When feelings come up again or for what ever reason you may find your self in a slip-up or fall-back in a situation with this person and no matter how bad it is, you cannot stay away. You must make a confession to fall out of agreement with them, him, her, and/or it, **by name**.

There is a process to deliverance, a process to freedom, and **you deserve to be free**. I'm not gonna say it's super easy but it is possible. I am healed from every bad relationship that was toxic in my life only by the power of Yeshua at work in me and doing my part to stay free. And I fight to stay free, you will too.

At any given moment something can trigger the bad side of me. And I must continue to fall out of agreement .

We must fall out of agreement with the sin areas and agree with what God has written in HIs word about us. Agree with the blessings of God, the peace of God, and the freedom in God.

Make the decision today! Decree, "I will no longer agree with what is not supposed to be attached to my true identity!"

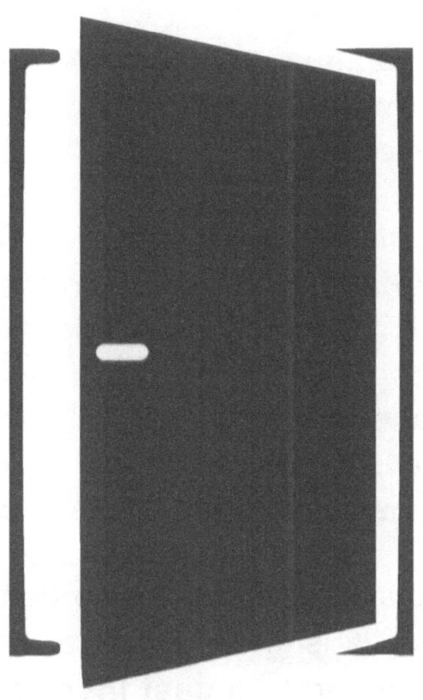

CHAPTER THREE

DELIVERANCE

"And they overcame him by the blood of the Lamb, and by the word of their testimony; and they loved not their lives unto the death."

Revelation 12:11

COME OUT OF HIDING: Activating Deliverance

What is deliverance? Merriam Webster defines it as the act of delivering someone or something. It is a state of being delivered; or liberation.

What is Deliverance Ministry? The casting out of demons or spirits in attempt to solve problems such as anger, fear, rejection, etc. Deliverance ministry also focuses on tearing down strong holds and anything that attempts to stand in God's place in your life. Spirits are not always easy to recognize. Most of the time, they are hiding, waiting for the right (wrong) time to manifest or come out.

Instead of playing a peek-a-boo game with bad spirits and bad behaviors, it is the goal of a warrior, a victorious believer, such as you and I, **to cast them out.**

Matthew 10:8 (NLT) says, "Heal the sick, raise the dead, cure those with leprosy, and **cast out demons.** Give as freely as you have received!"

Deliverance goes back to the Old Testament, where God raised up Moses to be a deliverer for the children of Israel in order that they may be free. Take some time and read The Book of Exodus chapter three. You will notice I have included a lot of scripture references, and it's on purpose, read every reference! The more of God's word you get inside of you, the easier it is to stay free. I want you to know today that freedom is your portion and one of the ways it comes is by the word of God.

John 8:36 says, "So if the Son sets you free, you will be free indeed!" Once you have been set free, make it your mission to help someone else come out of hiding and find their freedom. We must never forget to strengthen them that remain. Revelation 3:2 (ESV) says, "Wake up, and strengthen what remains and is about to die, for I have not found your works complete in the sight of my God."

Deliverance will not take place until you are honest enough to tell the truth. John 8:32 (NIV) states, "Then you will know the truth, and the truth will set you free." 2 Corinthians 1:3-4 (NIV) says, "Praise be to the God and Father of our Lord Yeshua (Jesus The Christ), the Father of compassion and the God of all comfort, who comforts us in all our troubles, so that we can comfort those in any trouble with the comfort we ourselves receive from God."

First, identify what you are dealing with or something, of which, you desire to be free. Next, identify the only One who can set you free, that is, Yeshua. Then, identify who God is to you. If you do not have a relationship with The Father, you need to say the following prayer first. Once you have accepted Yeshua into your heart and life, you will then have access to the saving power, healing, deliverance, miracles, signs, and wonders that accompany the believer!

Romans 10:9 (KJV) 9 "That if thou shalt confess with thy mouth the Lord Jesus (Yeshua), and shalt believe in thine heart that God hath raised him from the dead, thou shalt be saved."

Say this prayer:
"Lord, I repent for all the things that I have done that were not pleasing to your will. I'm sorry for my sins. Please forgive me and come into my heart. I believe that God sent Yeshua, His Son, to die for me. Today I confess with my mouth and believe in my heart that Yeshua is Lord. Thank you for saving me!"

Just like that you have gained access. All things are possible, only believe. Now you have access! Let's continue.

SPIRITUAL DELIVERANCE

Spiritual deliverance is the activity of cleansing a person from evil spirits in order to address problems manifesting in that person's life. Often, these problems are a result of the presence of evil or root causes which require a person to be 'set' free. Root causes lie beneath the surface. Root causes reveal what brought about a particular behavior, bad habit, old paradigm, series of thoughts, or strong holds. There is always a beginning, and, there is always a root. The challenge is finding and identifying the root.

A tree flourishes or dies by the health of the root.

The root is the strongest part of a tree. The foundation of the tree is not seen on the surface, but all the nutrients are pass through the tree from the top to the bottom via the roots. The tree flourishes or dies by the health of the root. Once a root goes bad the tree will eventually die or fall.

Spiritually, if you don't address the root of a strong hold, mindset, or bad habit, you too, will take a fall and possibly die. A strong hold is spiritual bondage. It is a fortified place in the mind, soul, or even one's emotions.

Prayers of deliverance are designed to set a person free from bondage. There are times we may not even be aware we are bound, don't believe we are bound, or we may have become comfortable with being bound. Galatians 5:1 reads, "It is for freedom that Christ has set us free. Stand firm, then, and do not let yourselves be burdened again by a yoke of slavery." The Gospel of John 8:36 declares, "So if the Son sets you free, you will be free indeed." Galatians 5:13 states, "You, my brothers and sisters, were called to be free. But do not use your freedom to indulge the flesh; rather, serve one another humbly in love."

A while ago, I was was praying with a young lady to receive freedom and deliverance from a spirit of suicide that had come upon her. This spirit did not come alone it was a result of a strong hold of rejection. The rejection had become a trigger for emotional bondage that followed her into every relationship she was drawn too. The more she gave of herself, the more she was hurt. The rejection, sorrow, bitterness, and loneliness, all brought her to a place of hopelessness which caused depression. This depression created suicidal thoughts and began to take over her mind and emotions. I had been there, so I was able to recognize the attack. In praying with her, she began to say no. I can't! No I won't! This "no" was the stronghold at work. I would pray fervently and decree "spirits of suicide go in the name of Yeshua." She was saying "I can't!" But, with authority I said, "You can and you will come out!" There is power and authority in the name of Yeshua, and no matter how bad a person is under attack, if that individual desires to be free, their desire must be greater. The power of God will override the flesh and they <u>will</u> be set free. After praying for about an hour, she was set free!

Keep in mind, every deliverance case is different. Some people will instantly be free and others will experience a process to their freedom. All that is negative may come at you attempting to keep you chained until it seems as if a heavy load is upon you. "But, thanks be unto God who has given us the victory!" There have been times in my life when I had to pray to the Father to be delivered from toxic relationships (with people, alcohol and even food). You have to make a decision and desire a life-change in every area.

When I did, I fell out of agreement with sin in all areas of my life: mental, physical, spiritual, and emotional. I have learned to **practice freedom daily**. The prayer or prayers of deliverance are not a one time deal. You must actively keep the faith and attitude of freedom. Much like a cigarette smoker, food addict, or pornography addict, you have to know that Yeshua's work on the cross has made you free. However, you must put in the work and discipline to maintain a lifestyle change. **With deliverance comes responsibility.** Responsibility to change, shift an old paradigm, and truly turn away from everything which is not like God. This allows you to walk towards victory.

You owe it to yourself to remain free. If depression ever tries to come upon me, I can make the decision to stay chained to it, or I can fight for my joy and freedom! Prayers of deliverance will stir up the faith necessary to stand against the attack of the enemy. Praying for someone who has a strong spirit of bondage is not an easy task. But, when the people you are praying and believing for are ready—no weapon formed against them will prosper.

> **You must put in the work to maintain freedom.**

Dealing with deliverance is a serious subject. **You must desire change.** There must be a desperation for freedom. I have been set free in many areas. I have seen many people set free. None of these triumphs occurred until desperation created action. One of the most important parts of this action is CONFESSION. You must address your enemy by name. Fear, rejection, procrastination, insecurity, pride, shame, etc. What is holding you back? Command it to let go!

You must be completely honest with yourself, God, and any spiritual mentors assigned to you. Do not be afraid to address your struggles by name. They are illegally trespassing in a temple (you) that belongs to God. Serve an eviction notice to every struggle to come out of hiding and command everything not like God to GO!

When a lifestyle of deliverance is the goal:

CHART: SIX STEPS TO FREEDOM

○ **STEP ONE: Acceptance**

○ **STEP TWO: Confession**

○ **STEP THREE: The process of freedom is the bridge.**

○ **STEP FOUR: Patience is the fuel.**

○ **STEP FIVE: Consistency is the maintenance.**

○ **STEP SIX: Freedom is at the finish line.**

Finish Strong!

When life vs. death is the only option, CHOOSE LIFE!

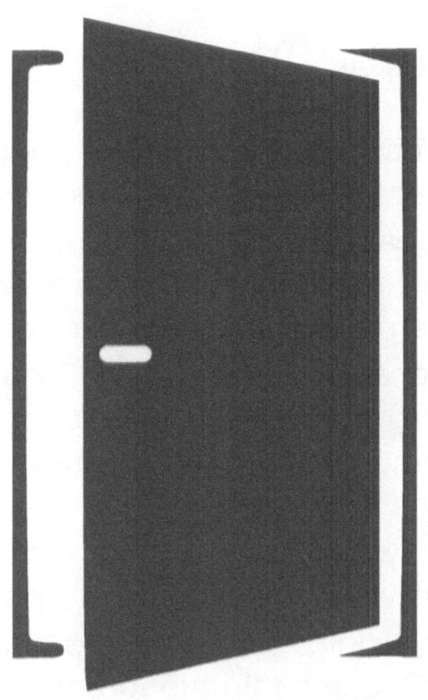

CHAPTER FOUR

WHO IS GOD TO YOU?

"And they overcame him by the blood of the Lamb,
and by the word of their testimony; and they loved
not their lives unto the death."

Revelation 12:11

Religion vs Relationship

When Yeshua ministered to the people he went to the ones who were usually outcasts, the most sick, hurting, sometimes even dead on arrival . But their condition did not stop his ability to heal nor did their condition cause him to reject them, this is relationship. He truly cared for the people and he expressed this . Matthew 9:36 states, "But when Yeshua saw the crowds, he felt pity for them, for they were weary and wandering, like sheep without a shepherd."

Yeshua always pointed out the fact, it's not what you do to be seen, but what actions you do because it's in your heart to do right. Religion causes us to behave a certain way to get attention. Relationship alone commands the attention of heaven and causes us to look like our Messiah. Matthew 23:25-26 reads, "25 You Pharisees and teachers are show-offs, and you're in for trouble! You wash the outside of your cups and dishes, while inside there is nothing but greed and selfishness. 26 You blind Pharisee! First clean the inside of a cup, and then the outside will also be clean.

Pharisees only believe in the strict law only concerned with following it to the letter ,however we serve a God who is rich in mercy and God promised us that Goodness and Mercy follow us . It is   by Grace we are saved not because of any law we are good enough to keep, there is no one good. For all have sinned and fallen short of the Glory of God. "Love, mercy and truth purge the heart of sin" (Proverbs 16:6). It is not your works that make you holy, your clothes, make up or your church denominations , that's religious thinking.   It's your faith and actions that bring us to repentance and strengthen the relationship with the father.

The Pharisees

WHO IS GOD TO YOU

Phar·i·see noun
1. a member of an ancient Jewish sect, distinguished by strict observance of the traditional and written law, and commonly held to have pretensions to superior sanctity.
    ○ a self-righteous person; a hypocrite.

The Pharisees claimed to know the law,Moses law (Torah) but did not recognize God in flesh ? How ironic. Religion doesn't have the ability to tap into spiritual discernment. Where religion began , the spirit of God was but soon got drowned out by man's agenda and self righteousness in effort to keep the law, there was a lack for the creator of the law. Paul states to us in Romans 2:13 (CJB) "For it is not merely the hearers of Torah whom God considers righteous; rather, it is the doers of what Torah says who will be made righteous in God's sight."

There is not one of us who will please God by being good. There is no good in mankind. But God sent his son (relationship), to die for all mankind for eternity, (relationship) to remove the stain of sin and death, (Relationship) and then rise from death with all power ,to sit at the right hand of the Father and continuously make intersession for mankind. What a powerful Relationship. Religion is not tangible. Religion separates the body. Relationship is birthed from love. Oh how the Father loves us! Stop judging your brothers and sisters because of a flaw or proclivity this is Pharisee behavior. Instead pray for the same Grace to abound that found you. Deliverance is for everyone just like salvation is for all who call on the name Of Yeshua.

Long story short, the Pharisees expected their "savior of the Jews" to be as passionate at keeping the law as they were. However Yeshua wanted them to awaken to the reality that their God,God of Abraham ,Isaac, Jacob and Moses,sent

Yeshua, He was the Shalom they were praying and waiting for, and that his very presence fulfilled the law . He came to do away with religious practices and develop relationship. The proclamation in James 2:19, resounds, " You believe that God is one; you do well. Even the demons believe—and shudder!"

<u>A Pharisee Sarcasm</u>

Now there was a certain man among the Pharisees named Nicodemus, a ruler (member of the Sanhedrin) among the Jews, who came to Yeshua 'at night' (blind to the revelation of who Yeshua really was) and said to Him, "Rabbi (Teacher), we know [without any doubt] that You have come from God as a teacher; for no one can do these signs [these wonders, these attesting miracles] that You do unless God is with him." Yeshua answered him, "I assure you and most solemnly say to you, unless a person is born again [reborn from above--spiritually transformed, renewed, sanctified], he cannot [ever] see and experience the kingdom of God." Nicodemus said to Him, "How can a man be born when he is old? He cannot enter his mother's womb a second time and be born, can he?" Yeshua answered, "I assure you and most solemnly say to you, unless one is born of water and the Spirit he cannot [ever] enter the kingdom of God. That which is born of the flesh is flesh [the physical is merely physical], and that which is born of the Spirit is spirit. (Relationship) Do not be surprised that I have told you, 'You must be born again [reborn from above--spiritually transformed, renewed, sanctified].' "For God so [greatly] loved and dearly prized the world, that He [even] gave His [One and] only begotten Son, so that whoever believes and trusts in Him [as Savior] shall not perish, but have eternal life (John 3:1-7, 16 AMP)."

A quote by Paul Washer states, "[Alot of people] think that Christianity is you doing all the righteous things you hate and avoiding all the wicked things you love in order to go to Heaven. No, that's a lost man with religion. A Christian is a person whose heart has been changed; they have new affections." When your heart has changed you have encountered a relationship.

The scribes and the Pharisees brought a woman taken in adultery. Having set her in the middle, they told him, "Rabbi, we found this woman in adultery, in the very act. Now in our Torah, Moses commanded us to stone such women. What then do you say about her?" They said this testing him, that they might have something to accuse him of. But Yeshua stooped down and wrote on the ground with his finger. But when they continued asking him, he looked up and said to them, "He who is without sin among you, let him throw the first stone at her." Again he stooped down and wrote on the ground with his finger. They, when they heard it, being convicted by their conscience, went out one by one, beginning from the oldest, even to the last. Yeshua was left alone with the woman where she was, in the middle. Yeshua, standing up, saw her and said, "Woman, where are your accusers? Did no one condemn you?" She said, "No one, Lord." Yeshua said, "Neither do I condemn you. Go your way. From now on, sin no more.(Yochanan 8:3-11 WMB)"

Religion will box you into a system of doing things one way. Relationship gives us the ability to be close to God. Religion is usually fueled by ignorance. Relationship creates individuality, which allows the believer to know God intimately for himself. As leaders it's important to teach the believer how to know and hear God for themselves intimately. And to express the importance of a relationship with the Father. Your struggle may not be the lust of the flesh, lust of the eyes or the pride of life. Perhaps pride and prejudice, bitterness or unforgiveness, being so quick to judge others wrongs that you forget about not always having it together? This is toxic as well. You see the Pharisees didn't even care that there were sick amount them that needed the touch of the Messiah. They got caught up in not approving of what he looked like? We must be careful that seeing we don't see or hearing we still never truly hear.

Let's consider the following texts:

Matthew 9:9-13 (WMB)
As Yeshua passed by from there, he saw a man called Matthew sitting at the tax collection office. He said to him, "Follow me." He got up and followed him. As he sat in the house, behold, many tax collectors and sinners came and sat down with Yeshua and his disciples. When the Pharisees saw it, they said to his disciples, "Why does your rabbi eat with tax collectors and sinners?" When Yeshua heard it, he said to them, "Those who are healthy have no need for a physician, but those who are sick do. But you go and learn what this means: 'I desire mercy, and not sacrifice,' for I came not to call the righteous, but sinners to repentance."

It's imperative that we as believers don't get comfortable in the four walls of a church building. And allow religion to take root. For there is a world full of people on the outside that deserve to know the price that was paid in order for us to have a real relationship with a real God. Yeshua walked the earth and many still didn't recognize or discern who he was , they missed their chance to have one on one time with the savior.

Yochanan (John)1:10-14, 17 WMB
He was in the world, and the world was made through him, and the world didn't recognize him. He came to his own, and those who were his own didn't receive him. But as many as received him, to them he gave the right to become God's children, to those who believe in his name: who were born not

of blood, nor of the will of the flesh, nor of the will of man, but of God. The Word became flesh, and lived among us. We saw his glory, such glory as of the one and only Son of the Father, full of grace and truth. For the Torah was given through Moses (Religious Order). Grace and truth were realized through Yeshua the Messiah (Relationship with God).

As soon as He was approaching [Jerusalem], near the descent of the Mount of Olives, the entire multitude of the disciples [all those who were or claimed to be His followers] began praising God [adoring Him enthusiastically and] joyfully with loud voices for all the miracles and works of power that they had seen, shouting, "Blessed (celebrated, praised) is the K ing who comes in the name of the Lord ! Peace in heaven and glory (majesty, splendor) in the highest [heaven]!" Some of the Pharisees from the crowd said to Him, "Teacher, rebuke Your disciples [for shouting these Messianic praises]." Jesus replied, "I tell you, if these [people] keep silent, the stones will cry out [in praise]!" As He approached Jerusalem, He saw the city and wept over it [and the spiritual ignorance of its people], saying, "If [only] you had known on this day [of salvation], even you, the things which make for peace [and on which peace depends]! But now they have been hidden from your eyes. For a time [of siege] is coming when your enemies will put up a barricade [with pointed stakes] against you, and surround you [with armies] and hem you in on every side, and they will level you to the ground, you [Jerusalem] and your children within you. They will not leave in you one stone on another, all because you did not [come progressively to] recognize [from observation and personal experience] the time of your visitation [when God was gracious toward you and offered you salvation] (LUKE 19:37-44 AMP)."

In our pursuit of Kingdom, Mega Churches, Titles, Religion, God. Let us remain sensitive to relationship. Sensitive enough to recognize our time of visitation. And when we do we receive the Father in all his Glory. Come out of hiding, watch and pray. There's soon to be another visitation. This time He's gonna crack the sky! Will you be ready or still looking for a sign?

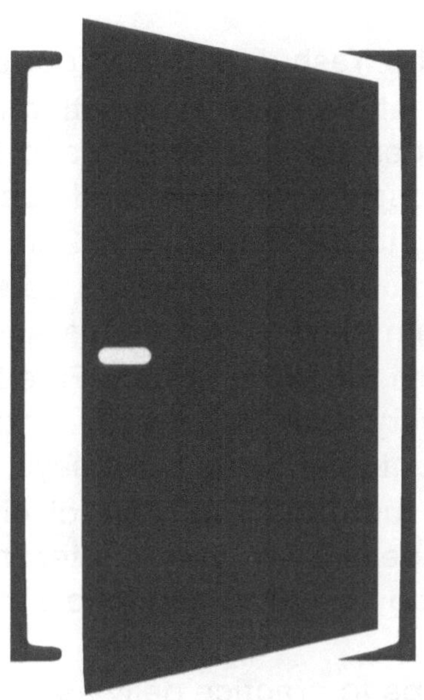

CHAPTER FIVE

YESHUA

"…Whosoever will come after me, let him deny himself, and take up his cross, and follow me."

Mark 8:34

Knowing who Yeshua is brings out a greater authority in you. Knowing that his spirit lives within us! And you have the authority to open up your mouth and bind the works of the enemy and loose the freedom and liberty you have as a result of belonging to the kingdom of God. When you belong to Yeshua, you are not just an average person, but a believer therefore a kingdom citizen, with rights and privileges of the kingdom. And in the Kingdom, we are Free from every yoke of bondage and slavery. (MARK 8:34-35) Knowing who Yeshua is makes us accountable! Gods word says, when Yeshua had called the people [unto him] with his disciples also, he said unto them, whosoever will come after me, let him deny himself, and take up his cross, and follow me."

Here are some steps to practice daily as a lifestyle:

STEP 1

DENY YOURSELF
Be lead of the spirit, sacrifice or give up the things that you know are not pleasing to God nor do they bring you closer to him, everything that looks, feels taste good is not good for you.

STEP 2

TAKE UP YOUR CROSS
Die out to the sins of the world. These are things which are against God: lifestyles, proclivities, practices, etc.

STEP 3

SACRIFICE FULLY UNTO GOD
Recognize your own need for God in your life and stick close to him. You must confess and believe, not my will but yours Lord be done in my life.

STEP 4

FOLLOW CHRIST
Become like Christ, follow his word his laws, learn his ways. Pay attention to how you live. Read and study the word of God, daily. Its not always easy, but by reading the bible and other spiritual reading material. We become more mature believers, strong in the faith and able to withstand temptations.

When we are following Yeshua we will not continue to be enticed by sin. I wish I could say there was an easy way, but as long as you are living this life at times will be enticed with sin. The good news is, there is a way out a way to freedom. And its Deliverance. If you are reading this manual, it's a clear indication that you are ready to **come out of hiding,** you want desperately to be free.

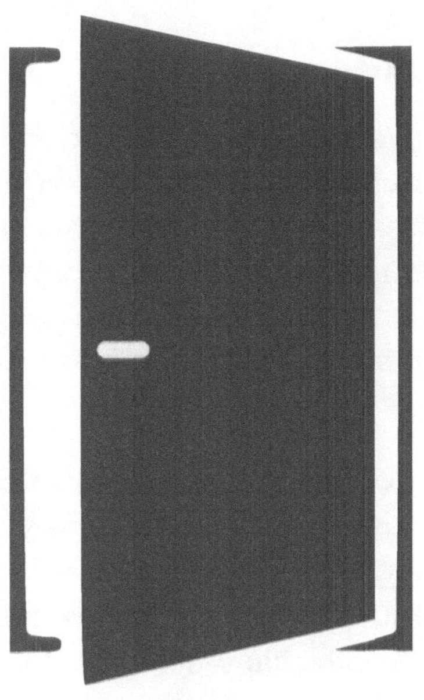

CHAPTER SIX

COME OUT OF HIDING

"8 For he said unto him, Come out of the man, thou unclean spirit. 9 And he asked him, What is thy name?…"

Mark 5:8-9

Come Out Of Hiding

Pray the prayers of deliverance in this book daily. If you belong to a local church, get to the alter at all cost. forget being embarrassed your freedom depends on this breakthrough. Maybe you need to find someone you trust to pray with you, someone who is stronger than you to help you get free. However, the prayers in this manual are easy and effective to pray alone as well.

Everyone's deliverance is different. Some will cry, yell, laugh, yawn, some just by telling someone your area of struggle, you will receive your deliverance. silence is hiding, telling your testimony brings you freedom! **Come out of hiding.** I can remember struggling with many different issues, sexual sin, lust, overeating anger unforgiveness the list goes on. That's just it ,they were silent struggles until I got fed up and wanted freedom. I would have a list at church with me during alter call,for the person praying to call out all the names of the spirits holding me captive. I would not leave until I felt free. This may or may not work for you, find your WAY. You must get serious about your freedom. You must desire more than anything to **come out of hiding,** and let your secrets be exposed in order that you can truly become Gods original opinion of you. I know it isn't always easy to be vulnerable and you can't tell everybody your secrets, but you can tell somebody. And you can absolutely tell your father God.

It's also important to prepare for deliverance. You must prepare your mind and your body fasting and prayer is a key to set the captives free.   Matthew 17:14-21 King James Version (KJV) "14 And when they were come to the multitude, there came to him a certain man, kneeling down to him, and saying, 15 Lord, have mercy on my son: for he is lunatick, and sore vexed: for ofttimes he falleth into the fire, and oft into the water. 16 And I brought him to thy disciples, and they could not cure him. 17 Then Yeshua answered and said, O faithless and perverse generation, how long shall I be with you? how long shall I suffer you? bring him hither to me.18 And Yeshua rebuked the devil; and he departed out of him: and the child was cured from that very hour.19 Then came the disciples to Yeshua apart, and said, Why could not we cast him out? 20 And Yeshua said unto them, Because of your unbelief: for verily I say unto you, If ye have faith as a grain of mustard seed, ye shall say unto this mountain, Remove hence to yonder place; and it shall remove; and nothing shall be impossible unto you.21 Howbeit this kind goeth not out but by prayer and fasting." King James Version (KJV)

For the purpose of this context Fasting is abstaining from something, possibly negative or habitual, with the concentration on something positive or meditating on God's word and spending time in prayer. Giving up of things that mean something to you or you enjoy, for the sake of giving it as an offering that will honor God. There are many different effective ways to fast. You may fast from food, sweets, soda, snacks, certain meal times. You can fast social media, telephone, certain past times. When I fast, I try to deny myself of anything pleasurable. Sometimes I fast for a few hours in a day and sometimes I fast for days. It depends on how bound I am or how bad I want to be set free. Or just how bad I want more of God. So, I give my fasting as an offering that I may be cleansed from the inside out. I make sure I set aside time to pray and read my bible. However you choose to sacrifice, it's up to you, but to see results you must prepare for deliverance and the sacrifice of fasting is very effective.

<u>Come Out</u>

Whatever your dealing with, call it by name and tell it to go! Command it to **Come out of hiding** and for once and for all bee free. Luke 4:35 "Be quiet!" Yeshua said sternly. "Come out of him!" Then the demon threw the man down before them all and came out without injuring him."

Mark 5:6-6 When he saw Yeshua from a distance, he ran and fell on his knees in front of him. 7 He shouted at the top of his voice, "What do you want with me, Yeshua Son of the Highest God? In God's name don't torture me!" 8 For Yeshua said to him, **"Come out** of this man, your impure spirit!" 9 Then Yeshua asked him, "What is your name?" "My name is Legion," he replied, "for we are many." 10 And he begged Yeshua again and again not to send them out of the area."11 A large herd of pigs was feeding on the nearby hillside. 12 The demons begged Yeshua "Send us among the pigs; allow us to go into them." 13 He gave them permission, and the impure spirits came out and went into the pigs. The herd, about two thousand in number, rushed down the steep bank into the lake and were drowned."

There is Power in the name of Yeshua! Whether you struggle in one area or many areas, today is a great day to be free. What are you hiding? Take authority over it today. Find a quiet place and pray that you may be free. Deliverance brings freedom. Deliverance is for you and me, **come out of hiding** it's time to be free! Pray these prayers.

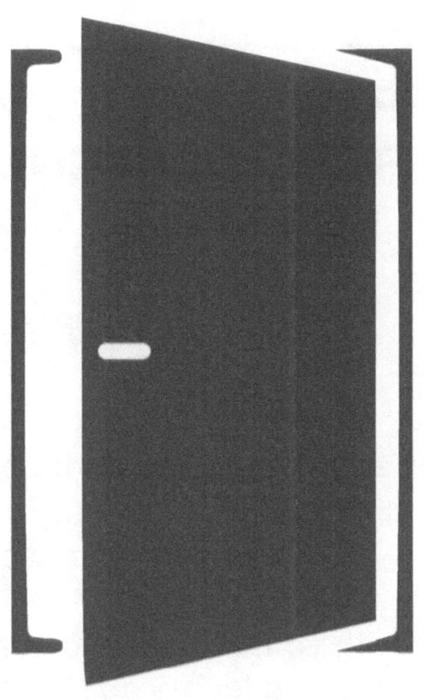

CHAPTER SEVEN

GATEWAY TO FREEDOM!

This chapter is an outline of prayers for you to pray daily, or, as often as you need. Be diligent! Be Fervent! This is a matter of your freedom. God wants you free and I want you free. However, you are the only one who can make this happen. DO IT!

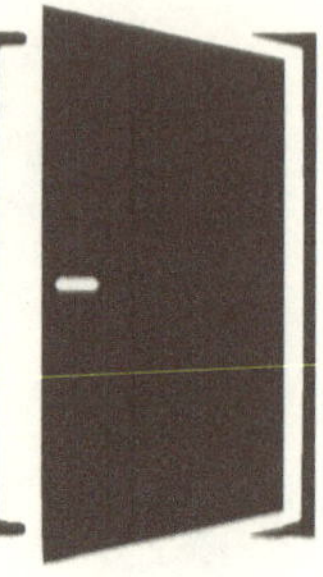

PRAYER OF DELIVERANCE FROM ADDICTION
- ## Read Matthew 11:28-30

Today I fall out of agreement with spirits of addiction. All addictions holding me back I identify you by name. _____________________ (state your addiction/s aloud)

I no longer agree with you. I command every spirit of addiction to loose me and let me go NOW—In the Name of Yeshua.

I brake all covenants that I or my ancestors made with you. I fall out of agreement with all behaviors, actions, people, places, and things that trigger me to go towards my weakness.

Today I command every spirit of addiction to come out of hiding, manifest and GO! Never to return in the Name of Yeshua.

Come out of my memories, come out of my emotions in Yeshua's Mighty Name—Amen!

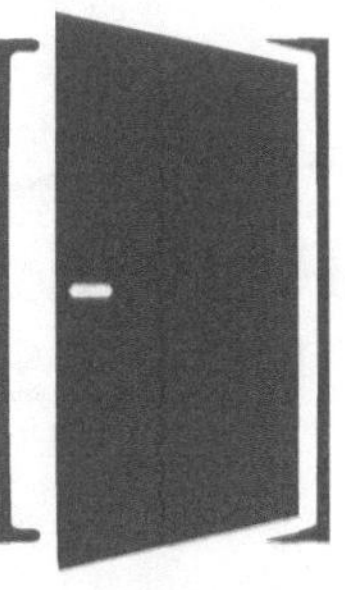

PRAYER OF DELIVERANCE FROM MENTAL TORMENT
• Read Philippians 2:5-11

Today I fall out of agreement with spirits of mental torment, mental illness and thoughts of suicide.

All mental strongholds attempting to rob me of my freedom—I bind you in the Name of Yeshua, and, I command you to loose your hold of my mind, my will, and my emotions. I identify you by name. I expose you. I command you to **GO** and no longer torment me. **I have the mind of Christ**. I no longer agree with you.

I command every spirit of mental torment, mental illness, suicide, and all spirits connected to you to **GO** in Yeshua's Mighty Name. Loose my mind and let me go NOW in the Name of Yeshua.

I brake all covenants that I made or my ancestors made with you. I fall out of agreement with all behaviors, actions, people, places, and things that cause my mind to wander, daydream, or have a nightmare. I expose you.

Today, I command every spirit of torment to **come out of hiding,** manifest, **GO,** and never to return in the Name of Yeshua. Come out of my memories! Come out of my emotions! Come out of me in Yeshua's Mighty Name— Amen!

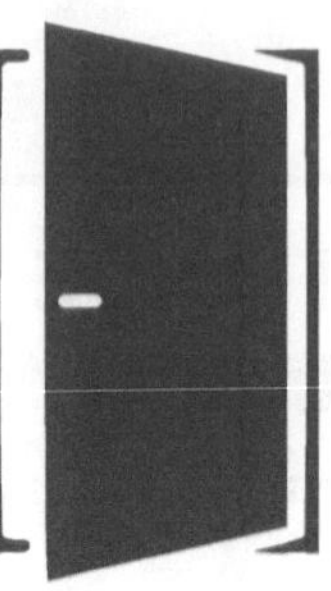

PRAYER OF DELIVERANCE FROM BAD RELATIONSHIPS
• Read Proverbs 13:20

Today I fall out of agreement with all ungodly relationships.

All relationships holding me back I identify you. I no longer agree with you.

I command every bad relationship to be severed at the root. Loose me and let me **GO NOW** in the Name of Yeshua.

I brake all covenants that I made with you. I fall out of agreement with all ungodly relationships that cause me not to grow and soul-ties that were sent from the enemy.

Today I command every spirit of insecurity to come out of hiding, manifest, **GO!** Never return in the Name of Yeshua.

I am worthy of a healthy relationship.

All bad relationships come out of my memories and emotions in Yeshua's Mighty Name—Amen!

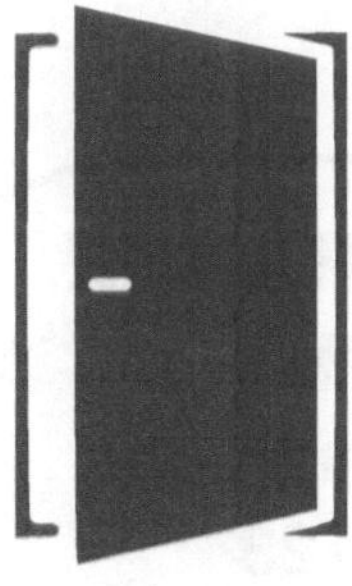

PRAYER OF DELIVERANCE FROM LONELINESS & DEPRESSION
- **Read Hebrews 13:5**

Today I fall out of agreement with spirits of loneliness and depression. All lies of the enemy holding me back, I identify you by name. Loneliness and depression **GO!** I no longer agree with you.

I command every spirit of loneliness and depression to loose me and let me **GO NOW** in the Name of Yeshua.

I expose you. Spirit of depression, you have no authority over me. The Joy of the Lord is my strength.

I brake all covenants that I made or my ancestors made with you. All spirits connected to my heritage or bloodline you are not welcome—I command you to go now in the Name of Yeshua.

I fall out of agreement with all behaviors, actions, people, places, and things that trigger me to go backward instead of forward. I will no longer be comfortable with feelings of loneliness; for GOD is always with me. I am not alone.

Today I command the spirit of loneliness and depression to come out of hiding, manifest, and GO! Never return in the Name of Yeshua. Come out of my mind, my will, and my emotions, in Yeshua's Mighty Name—Amen!

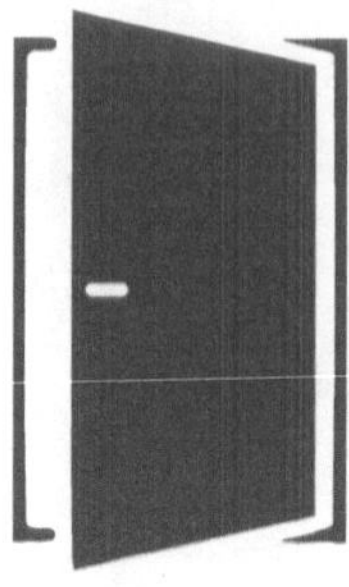

PRAYER OF DELIVERANCE FROM PORNOGRAPHY

- Read Job 31:1, 2 Corinthians 6:17, Colossians 2:21-23

Today I fall out of agreement with spirits of pornography.

All spirits of perversion holding me captive I expose you! I no longer agree with you! I command every spirit of pornography to loose me and let me **GO NOW** in the Name of Yeshua.

I brake all covenants that I or my ancestors made with you, and those connected to my bloodline. I fall out of agreement with all behaviors, actions, people, places, visuals, and other things that trigger me to go towards my weakness and away from freedom.

Today I command every spirit of perversion and every spirit of pornography to come out of hiding, manifest and **GO!** Never to return in the Name of Yeshua!

Come out of my memories! Come out of my emotions! I no longer desire you! I will no longer touch the unclean thing in Yeshua's Mighty Name—Amen!

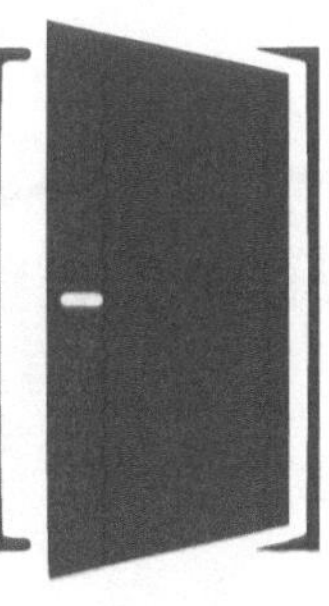

PRAYER OF DELIVERANCE FROM UNFORGIVENESS
• Read Matthew 6:9-15

Lord please forgive me as I forgive others. I fall out of agreement with the spirit of unforgiveness.

I will not continue to hold grudges against those who have wronged me. I will not hold someone's faults against them. I give it to you, Lord. Vengeance is yours.

I will not be bitter. I will be 'Better Than Before'. I ask that you would remove the burden , the hurt, the bitterness, and the sting of the memories.

Teach me to forgive. Today I let Go of
_________________________ , In the Name of Yeshua.

I let all anger, rage, bitterness, and unforgiveness go NOW, in the Name of Yeshua. I pray against every situation that left me in a place of unforgiveness. Please sever every ungodly soul tie and soul-connection at the root.

I declare my soul is free! Heal me, and I shall be healed: mind, body, soul, and spirit. I want to be forgiven! Today, I make the choice to forgive in Yeshua's Mighty Name— Amen!

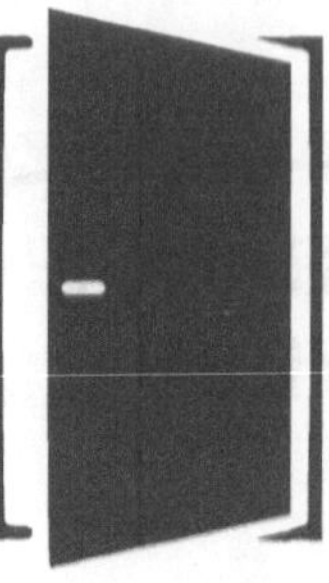

PRAYER OF DELIVERANCE FROM REJECTION

- **Read James 2:3; Luke 10:15; Romans 8:31**

I fall out of agreement with the spirit of rejection!

Rejection from men, rejection from women, rejection from mother, rejection from the father, rejection from the womb.

I command you to GO NOW, in the Name of Yeshua.

Spirits of sadness connected to rejection, you are exposed, and powerless against the power of God.

Rejection because of my size, my color, my gender, GO! Rejection from relationships, rejection from promotion, GO!

Every area of rejection, I command you to GO NOW, in the Name of Yeshua.

Rejection will not control me. I fall out of agreement with the spirit of offense connected to rejection. I am free, I am loved, I am no longer bound by rejection, in Yeshua's Mighty Name—Amen!

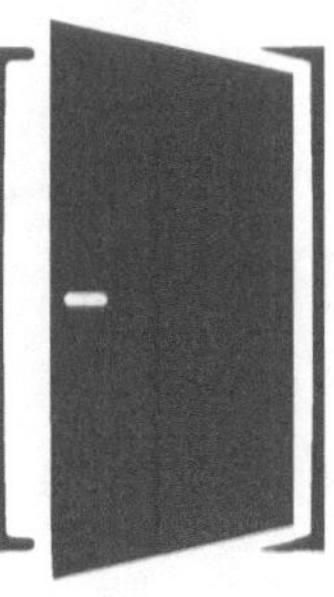

PRAYER OF DELIVERANCE FROM SPIRIT OF FEAR
• Read 2 Timothy 1:7

Today, I fall out of agreement with the spirit of fear!

God has not given me a spirit of fear, but of POWER, LOVE, and of a SOUND MIND.

Fear and every spirit connected to you, you will no longer have dominion over my mind. I command spirits of fear, worry, and anxiety, to GO NOW, in the Name of Yeshua.

I cast all my cares, worry, and anxiety on Yeshua. I am free from fear. My past does not control me. I am fearless.

Spirit of fear, you are exposed, and powerless against the power of God. Anxiety, you are powerless in the presence of God. I am free. I am fearless, in the name of Yeshua . Thank you, Lord, for freedom—in Yeshua's Mighty Name —Amen!

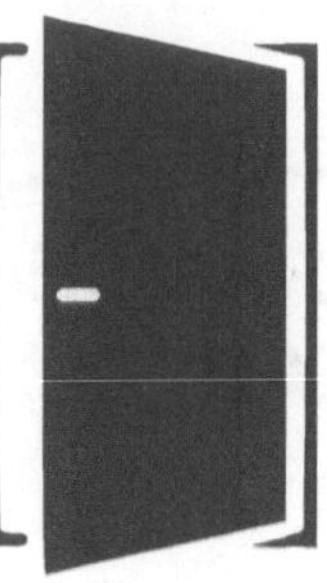

PRAYER OF DELIVERANCE FROM SPIRIT OF ABUSE
- Read Psalm 86:6 (NIV); Psalm 37:5-9 (MSG)

I fall out of agreement with the spirit of abuse. I will no longer be tormented. It was not my fault. I did not deserve it. I am not what happened to me. I will not become my abuser.

I am free. I am loved. I am whole. I am healed. God, please deliver me from the spirit of abuse. (Mental, physical, emotional or sexual).

I command the spiritual torment to GO NOW in the Name of Yeshua.

Lord, help me to release my abuser into Your hands, and heal me from the inside out. I will no longer be tormented by the spirit of abuse. The memories or nightmares of abuse. I do not agree with you anymore. I plead the Blood of Yeshua over my thought-life.

God help me find pure love in you, with out the stain of abuse hindering me from receiving your love. In the name of Yeshua I am free—in Yeshua's Mighty Name—Amen!

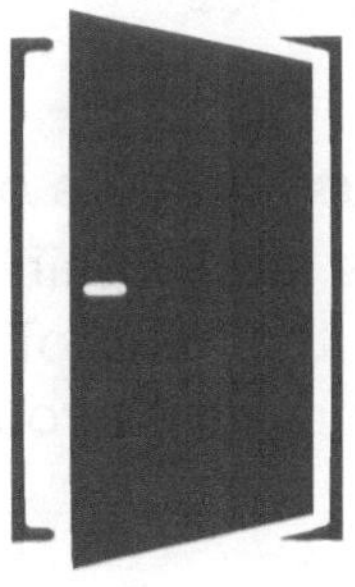

PRAYER OF DELIVERANCE FROM SPIRIT OF LACK

- Read Psalm 34:10 (ESV); Psalm 23:1 (ESV); Proverbs 10:22 (KJV)

I fall out of agreement with the spirit of lack and all spirits connected to it.

I command spirits of lack, poverty, and debt, to loose my finances now in the Name of Yeshua. I shall be a good steward of over finances. I shall sow into fertile ground, and look forward to harvest-time.

I shall set aside the tithe, first. I shall be honest with my increase. God grant me wisdom. I fall out of agreement with spirits connected to my bloodline concerning lack, poverty, debt and all spirits linked to them.

I am part of a royal priesthood—I am blessed.

I fall out of agreement with old paradigms concerning money, wealth, and finances. I agree that you Lord make me rich and add no sorrow to Your blessings.

I am a lender, not a borrower. My finances are free. I am a master builder. Wealth is my portion, in Yeshua's Mighty Name—Amen!

COME OUT OF HIDING: Activating Deliverance

These prayers are selected to get various "Prayers of Deliverance" activated in your life, prayer times, and within your spiritual walk with the Lord. Once you get the hang of it, I challenge you to create your own prayers dealing with your personal areas of struggle.

In what areas are you weak? What has been holding you hostage? What is stopping you from moving forward? You have the power, (through Yeshua) to receive your freedom today! Be strong in the Lord and the Power of His Might!

Use your Voice. My Apostle, Darren Thomas always reminds us (in our church family at Rebirth Church), we live in a voice-activated Kingdom. In other words, you must open your mouth, and use your voice to activate deliverance.

Apostle Darren also recently wrote a book entitled "Build It In Public!" I will quote some powerful words from its conclusion. He ends with this charge, and, I pass this same charge to you as your reading now.

> **"You have been chosen to be present in the Kingdom for such a time as this. You have a command on your life to Build. Do not fear—Build!**
>
> **Do not come to God with excuses—Build. The time signature of heaven is calling for builders to take position In Public NOW! Kingdom Come...Will Be Done....Come Out of Hiding and Build it in Public "**

Powerful! Deliverance sets you in a place of freedom to build. When you are free, there is no mental, physical, or emotional limitations that will be able to stop your progress. As you pray, you are building confidence, faith, and relationship with God. **Come out of Hiding and Build!**

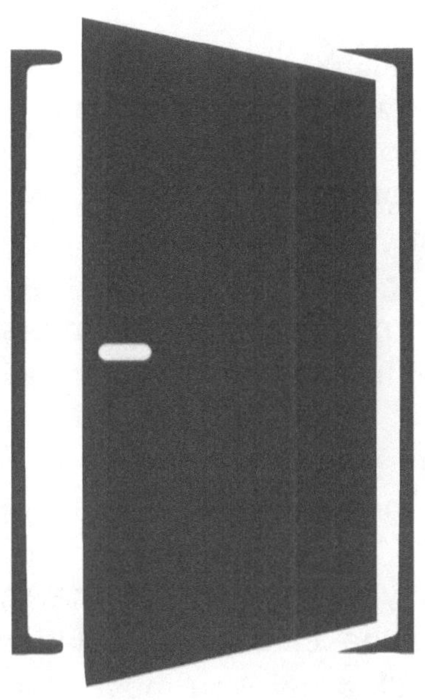

CHAPTER EIGHT

A NEW BEGINNING

"Therefore, if anyone is united with the Messiah, he is a new creation — the old has passed; look, what has come is fresh and new!"

2 Corinthians 5:17

The prayers listed in the previous chapter are just a few powerful prayers to get you started on your journey. Find someone to hold you accountable! Find someone walk with on your freedom journey. I hope this book will become a quick tool to assist you in finding the words to pray when you feel overwhelmed or not like yourself. Say these prayers and use them as a road map to guide you in praying powerful and effective prayers of freedom and deliverance.

You must do your part. After you pray these prayers, after you have left the altar, you <u>must</u> do your part.

The places you used to go that caused you to be tempted—the bar, the club, toxic relationships, etc,—from those you **must** walk away. You must part with friends (male and female) that are a negative influence on your freedom. Even music can mentally take you to a bad head-space. You must surrender those mediums (cd's, mp3's, etc.) and discard them. You simply cannot afford to listen them any longer.

Another great tool in maintaining your deliverance is seeking some sort of counseling. Counseling is provision of assistance and guidance in resolving personal, social, or psychological problems and difficulties, especially by a professional. Finding a Christian counselor would be great! However, a clinical counselor is helpful as well. Just seek help when life is seemingly too much to handle. There are a number of online counseling services available, as well as, sites for other outside resources that can help you in a location somewhere near you. Pray and ask God to guide you in the best direction.

When you are tempted to pick back up bad habits, you must find somewhere else to put that energy. Finding a local church to get involved in is an excellent tool. You can also find a clean hobby or read books. Fill yourself up with the word of God so there will be no empty or dry place in you (Ephesians 5:26).

We must stay clean and keep evil spirits out (Luke 11:24-26). Read your word. Find an accountability partner, someone who will speak positive into your life when negative thoughts come. Someone who will pray with you, someone who will love you thru a bad day someone who will listen someone who will be honest. Begin to journal. Write a book! Re visit that talent, dream, vision, idea that you may have put down, set long and short-term goals of where you want to be, what you want to accomplish. You must avoid at all cost the things, people places that hinder, tempt, or provoke you to want to go back into hiding. Be intentional. If you have a church home reach out to your pastor or someone with integrity among the church leadership to talk to. You don't have to suffer alone. Also seek out a good bible base church, there is always one somewhere near you seek and you shall find!

Remember whenever the enemy wants to try to stop your progress he will bring up your past. He doesn't understand your future so he deals in your past. But the past is under the blood! And in Christ future victory is sealed. So, whether the trauma happened in childhood, teenage years adulthood or even during church fellowship, yes even" church hurt "has to **Go.** God's desire is for you to be healed and set free. So, ignore all the instant replays in your mind the devil tries to embellish. The adversary is today and forevermore a liar and the father of lies! It is so...

Isaiah 38:16-17 declares, "Your words and your deeds brings life to everyone, including me. Please make me healthy and strong again it was for my own good that I had such hard times. But your love protected me from doom in the deep pit, and you turned your eyes away from my sins."

When you take responsibility for your life or relationship with God (or lack thereof), know the God loves you very much and is waiting for you to choose him. He will restore everything and anything that has been taken from you and heal you from the inside out! It won't happen overnight but when you go to him in prayer, suddenly your bands will loose and you will be free (Acts 16:26).

Finally, recite this prayer, "Dear heavenly Father, I pray that as You deliver me and continue to set me free little by little, day by day, that I will be sealed and covered by the blood of Yeshua that was shed on Calvary. I am free. I choose to be free. I walk in victory. The power of Christ is inside of me. Every prayer I prayed is sealed by The Blood of Yeshua,—The Resurrected One. I am healed and no longer broken.   I am delivered and no longer bound. I AM SET FREE in Yeshua's Mighty Nam—Amen.

Pray the prayers daily.   Pray with someone who is steeped and mature in prayer and their walk with God. Watch your life begin to transform as your mind is renewed!

Thank you for reading this book. May the Shalom of God surround you daily, this is my prayer. Feel free to invite me to your church for a freedom gathering.   It is time to operate "better than before!" It is time to heal. It is time to be set free. It is time to **Come Out of Hiding!**

Not the end...this is your beginning.

JOURNAL

JOURNAL

65

JOURNAL

JOURNAL

JOURNAL